Contents

The game of rugby   6

The pitch and positions   8

Catching and handling   10

Passing   12

Beating your opponent   14

Tackling   16

Kicking   18

The set scrum   20

Lineouts   22

Scoring and penalties   24

Tag rugby   26

Glossary   28

Further reading   29

Further information   29

Index   30

The game of rugby

Rugby is a fast and exciting game and is played all over the world. There are two forms of the game – rugby union and rugby league. In this book we will look only at rugby union.

Rugby union is a 15-a-side game played over two halves of 40 minutes each. The game is played with an oval ball, which can be kicked or passed. The aim of the game is to score points either from **tries** (touching the ball down over the opponents' goal-line) or by kicking the ball between two goal posts (see pages 24-25).

Kit

Rugby players usually wear long-sleeved rugby shirts and shorts. They are made of very strong material as they get a lot of tough wear. Each team has its own design for shirts. Players also wear long socks, held up with elastic garters and lace-up boots with studs.

Mouthguard

Shoulder pads

Rugby shirt

Gloves

Shorts

Socks

Boots

Because rugby is such a physical game, other protective items of kit are worn. These include mouthguards, gloves, shoulder pads and sometimes a **scrum cap** (left).

The pitch and positions

A full-sized rugby pitch is 100m long and 69m wide. On each goal-line is a set of goalposts with a bar. The ball must be kicked over the bar to score a goal. A halfway line crosses the middle of the pitch and touch lines mark the sides. Each team defends their own half.

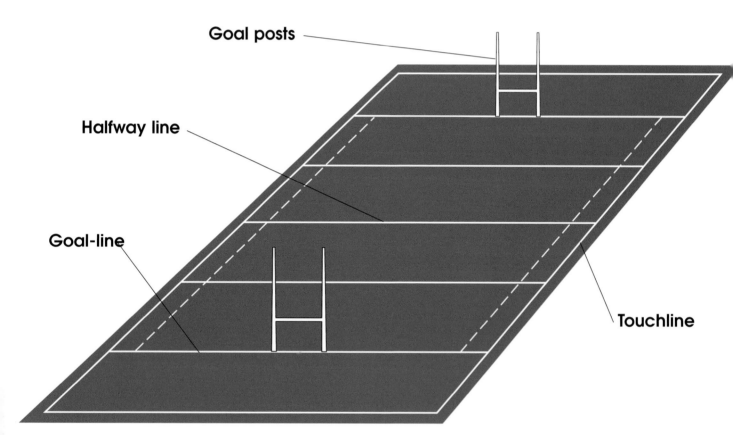

Goal posts

Halfway line

Goal-line

Touchline

The game of rugby includes a wide variety of activities. The ball can be caught, thrown, kicked and run with. If an opponent has the ball, you can tackle, push, pull, or try to wrestle it from him. Each player has a different role to play in the game.

The players

A rugby team is made up of eight **forwards** and seven **backs**.

The eight forwards make up the pack. Their job is to win possession of the ball through **scrums**, and **mauling** and **rucking**. Then they pass the ball to the backs who will attempt to get past the opponents.

The seven backs are made up of a scrum half, a fly half, two centres, two wings and a full back. They must pass the ball, and try to avoid tackles. Then they attempt to touch down the ball over the opposition's goal-line to score a try.

9

Catching and handling

Good catching skills are very important in rugby. If you fumble the ball, and knock it forwards, you will give away possession. This is called a **knock-on**.

You should aim to catch the ball at chest height in front of you. Your fingers should be spread and the ball should be caught close to your body. As soon as you have the ball you are likely to be tackled. You must hold the ball tight to stop the opposing players from taking it.

Ball handling skills - Catching

In a training session it is good to practise all areas of ball handling. To practise catching, arrange your team in a circle and throw the ball across the circle. Make sure the throws are all different – some low balls and some high.

Catching a high ball

A kicked ball is likely to travel high and be harder to catch.
1. You should spread your feet for balance (below) and raise your arms, fingers spread.

2. As the ball reaches you, bring your arms down and catch it against the chest (above).

Passing

Throwing or passing the ball is what makes rugby different from other football games. A player with the ball can only pass the ball backwards or sideways, never forwards. If the ball is passed forwards the referee will award a scrum to the other side. Teammates must run in support of the player with the ball and get in a position to receive.

1

2

There are three main stages of a pass:

1. Look for a player to pass to.

2. Swing the ball across your body.

3. Release the ball at the right time.

3

Ball handling skills – Passing

Many players find it easier to pass in one direction than the other. You need to be able to pass in both directions, so you can never have too much passing practice.

Using 6-8 friends, line up as you would on the pitch and pass the ball down the line as you all run forward. Make sure you throw the ball so your teammate can catch it easily. Only throw behind you.

Beating your opponent

A player with the ball must protect it and hold it with both hands to make it easier to pass in any direction.

Once you have the ball you have to decide what to do with it. If an opponent is about to tackle you, the best move is to pass the ball to a teammate. However sometimes you cannot do this and you need tactics to get past an opponent.

The sidestep

The sidestep tricks your opponent into thinking you are going one way, when in fact you go the other.

1. Put your weight on your left foot and look in that direction. **2.** As your opponent turns that way, shift your weight and push off in the other direction. Your opponent will be left going the wrong way.

The dummy pass

With the dummy pass you make your opponent think you are going to pass the ball to a teammate, but actually you keep hold of the ball and head off in another direction.

1. Look at your teammate and swing the ball towards him.

2. Your opponent will move toward your teammate to try and intercept the ball. You can then change direction and move the other way with the ball.

You have to look convincing to make this trick work and your teammate has to be prepared to support you.

Tackling

Tackling is an important part of rugby. Tackling must be done correctly so that nobody gets injured. A player can only tackle another player if he has the ball. The aim of the tackle is to stop the player with the ball and make him release the ball. A player on the ground must release the ball.

The side on tackle

The side on tackle is probably the most common tackle and the best one to learn first.

1. The tackler makes contact just above or below the waist.

2. He uses his body weight to unbalance the opponent. His head must go behind the player.

Rucks and mauls

Teams use rucks and mauls to try and keep possession of the ball after a tackle. In a ruck the ball is on the ground and the players must use their feet to ruck the ball backwards. It can then be picked up once it is out of the ruck. In a maul the ball is held off the ground and all the players must try to stay on their feet.

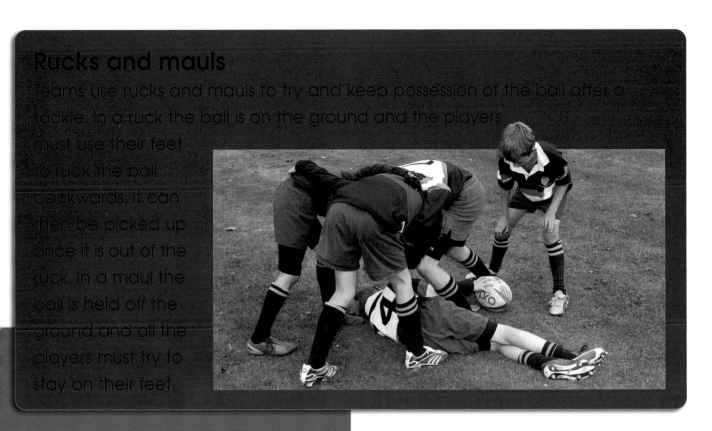

3. The tackler must wrap his arms firmly around the opponent's body and try to bring him to the ground.

Dangerous tackles

A dangerous tackle will be penalised with a **penalty**. Dangerous tackling includes tripping an opponent, tackling a player who no longer has the ball and high tackles around the neck or head.

Kicking

Kicking the ball can be done to gain ground (move further up the pitch) or to score points.

There are three main types of kick.

Punt kick

The **punt kick** is mainly used to move the ball up the pitch. The player drops the ball and kicks it before it reaches the ground. You cannot score a goal with a punt kick.

Drop kick

With a **drop kick**, the player drops the ball and kicks it just as it touches the ground. The player must keep his eyes on the ball and his weight on the non-kicking foot. This type of kick can be used to score a drop goal or to re-start a game.

Goal kick

The goal kick is used for **conversions** and penalty kicks (see pages 24-25) at the goal. To keep the ball steady place it on a **kicking tee**.

1. Start your approach from three or four paces away.

2. Keep your eye on the ball and swing your kicking leg back.

3. Kick the ball with your instep. The kick should follow through in front and slightly across your body.

The set scrum

A **set-piece** scrum is a way of restarting the game. This is called by the referee after a knock-on, a forward pass or other minor playing offence.

In a set scrum the two sets of forwards bind together in an organized formation.

The scrum

The scrum consists of:
Front row: 3 players: prop – hooker – prop
2nd row: 2 players: locks
Back row: 3 players: flanker – No.8 – flanker

The scrum half of the team who has been awarded the scrum puts the ball into the centre of the scrum. He will be hoping that his team's hooker will scoop the ball back with his feet through the forwards and back into play. The opposing hooker will also be trying to win the ball for his team.

The scrum half runs around the scrum to receive the ball. When he gets it he will either kick it or pass it to a team member, usually the fly half.

Lineouts

When the ball crosses the touchline at the side of the pitch it goes out of play. The referee will then call for another set-piece called a **lineout** to be formed.

The forwards of both teams line up where the ball went out. The two lines of players must be 1m apart. The hooker of the opposing team throws the ball down the middle of the line of players. He must try and throw the ball in so that his players have the best chance of catching it.

The throw must be straight or the referee will stop play and award a scrum. The players jump to try and catch the ball or knock the ball back to their scrum half.

Scoring and penalties

The winner of a rugby match is the team who has scored the most points. Points can be scored in four ways.

Tries

A try is worth five points. To score a try, a player has to touch the ball down on or behind the opposing team's goal-line. The ball must be placed on the ground, not dropped.

Conversions

When a player scores a try the team have the chance to add two extra points by kicking the ball between the posts and over the bar. This is called a conversion. The ball is kicked from any point along a line from the point where the try was scored.

Drop goals

A drop goal is scored by a player who succeeds in drop kicking the ball between the posts and over the bar at any stage of play. It can be scored from anywhere on the pitch and is worth three points.

Penalty kicks

A penalty kick is awarded to a team against whom the opposite team have fouled. The kick is taken from the point on the pitch where the foul was made. If it is in range of the posts a penalty goal can be scored with a place kick or a drop kick. This is worth three points.

Penalties

The referee can award a penalty if players break the rules. Here are a few referee's signals for penalties:

Knock-on – when the ball has been dropped or pushed forward.

Not releasing the ball immediately after a tackle, or holding onto the ball while on the ground.

High tackle – for tackles around the head or neck of another player.

Tag rugby

Because rugby is quite a physical game there is a fairly high chance of players getting hurt. To avoid this, younger players can play a non-contact version of the game called tag rugby.

In tag rugby there are usually between five and seven players on a team. Each player wears two ribbons tied to his or her waist.

A tackle occurs when a player manages to pull the ribbon away from a player on the opposite team. The tackler then steps back and the tackled player must stop and pass the ball.

Tag rugby can be played without scrums and lineouts and can be played on any surface. A try is worth one point and is scored by placing the ball on or behind the opponents' goal line.

Tag rugby is an ideal way to introduce rugby to both boys and girls. Many young players have enjoyed it so much that they continue to play as adults.

Tag rugby has become a popular game all over the world. This picture shows a match in India.

Glossary

backs the players who stand behind the scrum.

conversion the opportunity to get 2 extra points by scoring a goal after a try has been scored.

drop kick a kick when the ball is dropped and then kicked as it touches the ground.

forwards the players who form the scrum.

kicking tee a plastic stand that holds the ball in place for kicking.

knock-on when the ball touches a player and then moves forward up the pitch.

lineout the throw-in of the ball from the touchline to the lines of forwards.

mauling a way of regaining the ball after a tackle when the ball is held off the ground.

penalty awarding a team possession of the ball after the other team has committed a serious offence.

punt kick a kick of the ball made when the ball is dropped and kicked before touching the ground.

rucking a way of regaining the ball after a tackle when the ball is on the ground.

scrum cap a cap worn to protect a player's ears and head.

scrum a pushing contest between two sets of forwards; also the group name for the forwards.

set-piece a set way of restarting a game such as a scrum or lineout.

tries scoring five points by touching the ball down over the opposing team's goal-line.

Further reading

Rugby (Sporting Skills), Clive Gifford, Hodder Wayland, April 2008

Rugby (Inside Sport), Clive Gifford, Hodder Wayland, 2007

The Ultimate Guide to Rugby, Gavin Mortimer, Puffin Books, 2007

For the Love of Rugby (For the Love of Sports), Frances Purslow, Weigl Publishers, 2006

Rugby (Know Your Sport), Clive Gifford, Franklin Watts Ltd, 2006

Further information

It is easy to get started in rugby. To find out more you can contact the Rugby Football Union.

Rugby Football Union
Rugby House
Rugby Road
Twickenham
Middlesex
TW1 1DS
Website: www.england-rugby.com

Australian Sports Commission
PO Box 176
Belconnen ACT 2616
Australia
Website: www.ausport.gov.au

Australian Rugby Union
Ground Floor
29 - 57 Christie Street
St Leonards
NSW 2065
Australia
Website: www.rugby.com.au

Index

backs 9, 28

catching 10, 11, 12
conversions 19, 24, 28,

dangerous tackles 17,
   25
drop kicks 18, 24, 25
dummy pass 15

forwards 9, 20, 21, 23

gloves 7
goal kicks 19, 24, 25
goalposts 6, 8, 24, 25

high balls 11

kicking 8, 18, 19
kit 7
knock-ons 10, 20, 25, 28

lineouts 22-23, 28

mauls 9, 17, 28
mouthguards 7

passing 8, 12-13
penalties 17, 25, 28
penalty kicks 19, 25
pitch 8
possession 9, 10
punt kicks 18, 28

referee 20, 21, 23, 25
referee's signals 25
rucks 9, 17, 28

scoring 24-25
scrum caps 7, 28
scrums 9, 12, 20-21, 28
set pieces 20-21, 22-23,
   28

shoulder pads 7
side on tackle 16-17
sidestep 14

tackling 8, 16, 17
tag rugby 26-27
team 6, 9
tries 6, 9, 24